What's so funny about getting old?

Ed Fischer
and
Jane Thomas Noland

Meadowbrook Press
Distributed by Simon & Schuster
New York

Library of Congress Cataloging-in-Publication Data

Fischer, Ed
    What's so funny about getting old? / Ed Fischer and Jane
Thomas Noland.
        p.   cm.
    Originally published: Minneapolis, Minn. : CompCare
Publishers, c1991.
        1. Aging—Humor. 2. Old age—Humor. 3. Aged—Humor
I. Noland, Jane Thomas. II. Title
[PN6231.A43F57   1994]
741.5'973—dc20   94-25971
                                                                CIP

ISBN: 0-88166-223-2
Simon & Schuster Ordering # 0-671-51152-1

Cartoons and captions by Ed Fischer
Text by Jane Thomas Noland
Cover design by Jeremy Gale
Interior design by MacLean and Tuminelly

Published by Meadowbrook Press, 5451 Smetana Drive, Minnetonka,
MN 55343

BOOK TRADE DISTRIBUTION by Simon & Schuster, a division of
Simon and Schuster, Inc., 1230 Avenue of the Americas, New York,
NY 10020.

10   40 39 38 37 36 35 34 33

Printed in the United States of America

Why laugh?

Sages and others not so sage have come up with sayings to soften the experience of aging. "Older is wiser," they say. Even "older is better." We're inclined not to believe these elder Pollyannas—as our joints stiffen and our minds seem to have a mind of their own about what and what not to remember.

But there is one thing we've found to be true: older can be funnier! Only those of us who are "getting on" in years have the long view of life that allows us to see "what's so funny about getting old."

Now that we're past the earnestness of youth and the "acquisition years," when we took ourselves much too seriously, we're convinced that two things are absolutely essential in order to face the adventure of growing older: a healthy spirituality and a quick, robust sense of humor. In fact, humor can be a sign of a spiritual wellness!

Why this need for humor and laughter as we pass life's mid-mark?

Humor and laughter are good for our physical well-being—for all systems, from our immune to our cardiovascular. (Read Norman Cousins's *Anatomy of an Illness* or Allen Klein's *The Healing Power of Humor.*)

Humor helps us keep our balance when life deals us surprises.

Humor helps us communicate with younger generations.

Humor helps us make new friends and keep our old ones. Most people—no matter what their age—like to laugh. And they like the people they laugh with.

There's no doubt about it, humor can override the discomforts of advancing years. We believe that laughter actually can slow down the aging process.

We have a name for this new genre of humor for those of us who, as the euphemism goes, "aren't getting any younger": we call it "elderhumor."

So here is a little bookful of elderhumor—visual and verbal—observed and gathered by the coauthors, who, like everybody else, are getting older.

May *What's So Funny about Getting Old?* help you see the hum``or in your own situations and surroundings. May it lighten your outlook as it has ours!

Laughter, like hope, springs eternal, even as we're realizing that we, as aging mortals, are not. Tap into the wellsprings of elderhumor and grow old, if not gracefully, at least laughing all the way.

Jane Thomas Noland

"Old age is always fifteen years older than I am."
— Bernard Baruch

Social note from Sun City:

A seventy-two-year-old bride to her prospective matron of honor (age seventy-four): "Albert and I have decided to pool our assets."

Matron of honor: "You mean your two houses, your stocks and bonds, and your savings accounts?"

December bride: "No. Between us we have three good ears, two good eyes, two original hips (and two titanium facsimiles), three working knees, and most of our own teeth. Not a bad combination."

A younger generation redefines great-grandmother's health references:

DYSPEPSIA: withdrawal from Pepsi

CONSUMPTION: compulsive overspending

THE VAPORS: sinus trouble

THE GRIPPE: a bad back from carrying your own bags at the airport

CHILBLAINS: cold blains ("whatever THEY are!")

CATARRH: allergy to long-haired cats

SUMMER COMPLAINT: boredom

GLEAT: a chronic vibrato

if we're senior citizens, does that make everyone else Junior citizens?
ED FISCHER

Things not so important anymore toward the end of the alphabet:

Weekends
Waistlines
Winning

Blessings of age:

Confidential observation from a classy, nearly ninety
   dowager to a friend on a garden tour: "There's one
   good thing about being old—I almost never have to
   shave my legs anymore."

A question of usage:

Jenny, age sixteen, (asking): "Does 'chic sale*' have
   anything to do with designer jeans?"

Allison, age thirty-four, (guessing): "No, it's a French
   marketing strategy."

Marian, age eighty-seven, (knowing): "Actually, it's
   an outhouse."

*Named for Chic Sale, a vaudeville comedian who played
   to rural audiences, whose favorite routine was how to build
   an outhouse.

ED FISCHER

You know you're getting old when:

Your joints buckle and your buckles won't.

You resort to slip-on shoes.

The pucker marks around your mouth are not from puckering up.

You buy bras that fasten in front.

You discover an entirely new meaning to the word "unbending."

"Middle age is when anything new you feel is most likely to be a symptom."
— Laurence J. Peter, from *Peter's Quotations*

"Setting a good example for your children takes all the fun out of middle age."
— William Feather, from *The Business of Life*

"Middle age is when the girl you smile at thinks you are one of her father's friends."
— Henny Youngman

A child's view of retirement in a mobile home park:

After Christmas break, the teacher asked her small pupils how they spent their holiday. One little boy's reply went like this:

"We always spend Christmas with Granma and Granpa.

"They used to live up here in a big brick house, but Granpa got retarded and they moved to Florida.

"They live in a park with a lot of other retarded people.

"They all live in tin huts. They ride tricycles that are too big for me.

"They all go to a building they call the wrecked hall, but it is fixed now. They all do exercises but not very well. They play a game with big checkers and push them around on the floor with sticks.

"There is a swimming pool but I guess nobody teaches them. They just stand there in the water with their hats on.

"My Granma used to bake cookies for me, but nobody cooks there. They all go to restaurants that are fast and have discounts.

"When you come into the park, there is a doll house with a man sitting in it. He watches all day so they can't get out without him seeing them. I guess everybody forgets who they are because they all wear badges with their names on them.

"Granma says that Granpa worked hard all his life to earn his retardment. I wish they would move back home, but I guess the man in the doll house won't let them out."

Author unknown, submitted by Genrose Diorio

Staying in the race in spite of obstacles:

When your crinkles turn to wrinkles
and your wrinkles turn to seams,
when your nicely rounded bottom
is a widely flattened beam,
when you see your outsides changing
while your insides stay the same—
so old age won't overtake you,
KEEP ON RUNNING! That's the game!

J.T.N.

Brief exchange in a "total" beauty salon:

"Who spends half his time in a tanning booth and the
    other half at the cosmetic surgeon's?"

"I don't know. Who?"

"Friar Tuck."

You know you're getting old when:

You send your podiatrist a poinsettia for Christmas.

"I have everything now I had twenty years ago—except
    now it's all lower."

— Gypsy Rose Lee

Semantics:

When you're under fifty, you "collect."
When you're over fifty, you "amass."

Remember when:

You used to find fiber in your carpet—not in your
cereal bowl?

Older-than-thou one-upsmanship:

"I'm so old I was born back when knighthood was
in flower."

"I'm so old my prom date was Fred Flintstone."

You know you're getting old when:

You've seen five versions of *The Adventures
of Tom Sawyer* (1917, 1920, 1938, 1938, and 1972).

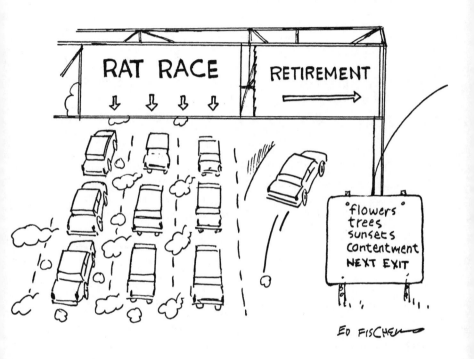

He knows he's getting old when:

He has the urge to pat Vanna White on the head.

Glacial drift:

"I'm getting on in years—probably should have moved
    south by now."
"High time. Parts of your body already have!"

Chronology—real and imagined:

"How old would you be if you didn't know how old
    you were?"

                             — Satchel Page

Mental fitness for midlifers and beyond:

When aging, very few men
will lose their acumen
if they continue to dabble
in crosswords and Scrabble.

                  J.T.N.

ED FISCHER

One old time-sharer to another:

"I'm too old to take turns."

More older-than-thou one-upmanship:

"I'm so old my great-great-grandfather was a tadpole."

"I'm so old my high school swim team did laps in the
      primordial pool."

One old dog-breeder to another:

"Is it true that after a while we begin to look like our
      pets?"

"Absolutely."

"Oh-oh. I'm going to sell the Shar Peis.*"

*A Chinese breed of dog known for its incredibly wrinkled skin.

Song to a mirror:

The face I see is furrowed now.
In fact, it's rather rutty.
Revlon and Clinique won't do.
I need a can of putty!

                    J.T.N.

Social guideline for seniors:

When names escape you,
just call everyone who looks familiar "Doc."

"By the time a man is wise enough to watch his step,
                    he's too old to go anywhere."
              — Joey Adams in *Strictly for Laughs*

Chronological clue:

Did you see Maud Adams or Mary Martin
        as "Peter Pan"?
If you saw Maud, you're very, very old.
If you saw Mary, you're pretty old too.

Unmet need:

"I don't need a Little Black Book anymore. I need a
BIG Black Book."

"Why?"

"To make room for all those names with the tacked on
initials—the M.D.s, C.P.A.s, L.S.W.s, and L.P.N.s."

Another unmet need:

"You know those magazines like *Playboy* and *Playgirl*—
I think they should have a *Playwoman* for us
seniors. For the centerfold, I'd vote for Maurice
Chevalier in his spats and boutonniere. Now *there*
was a ladies' man!"

Elderjoke:

Q.: What did the old tomcat say when the mice went
by on roller skates?

A.: Meals on wheels.

An elder who manages to live well on a shoestring suggests just a few economies to ease fixed-income budgets:

1. Use each tea bag three times.

2. Wash out and reuse all Baggies.

3. Share a communal *New York Times* with your neighbors. (Erase your penciled fill-ins on the crossword puzzle before passing it on.)

4. Save on laundry. Don't wear socks or undershirts (pantyhose or slips) except for the most demanding social occasion.

5. Be sure your golf guests reimburse you for their greens fees.

6. Buy generic kitty litter.

7. Hitch rides whenever possible with your friends.

8. Plan pricey dinner parties—and then find a sure-fire excuse to call them off at the last minute ("Sorry—I slipped a disc" or "My daughter had a baby"). But you'll at least get credit for trying.

9. Sew your wallet shut—or trade it for a coin purse.

10. Carry a deep handbag. By the time you've finished rummaging for your money, somebody else will have bought the tickets.

11. Dilute your shampoo and your dishwashing detergent.

12. And—clip coupons, clip coupons, clip coupons!

Sticker seen on a bumper in Palm Beach:

When I get old, I'm going to move north and drive slow.

> "If you survive long enough, you're revered—
> rather like an old building."
> — Katherine Hepburn

Moment of truth:

As the years add up
and the skin gets loose,
what I perceive as most distressing
is the little kid
who looks up at me
and says,"Lady,
you need pressing!"

J.T.N.

Experience:

"—a comb life gives you after you've lost your hair."
— Judith Stern

There are three major causes of old age: jobs, marriages, and kids—not necessarily in that order.

Comments heard in a retirement home corridor:

Ellin to her visiting niece, who was pushing her wheelchair, referring to a passing doctor: "Who was that?"

Niece: "I'm afraid I don't know him from Adam."

Ellin: "Who's Adam?"

Niece: "Oh, you know, Adam and Eve."

Ellin (looking up with a sly smile and offering this commentary on our times): "*They* can't still be together after all these years!"

"After the age of eighty, everything reminds you of something else."
— Lowell Thomas in *Time* magazine

"I used to dread getting older because I thought I would not be able to do the things I wanted to do, but now that I am older I find I don't want to do them."
— Nancy Astor

Interpretations:

SECURITY to a woman in her twenties means an advanced degree.

SECURITY to a woman in her sixties means a husband with a lot of life insurance or plenty of assets of her own.

SECURITY to a woman in her eighties means the guy with the hat and the badge who sits in the condo lobby.

Two neighbors in a retirement community talking about a third:

"All Henry does every day is monitor a relationship."

"What relationship? You mean he eavesdrops on those two who moved into 3C?"

"Oh, no. The relationship of his systolic to his diastolic."

You know you're getting old when:

You don't go anywhere without your sweater.

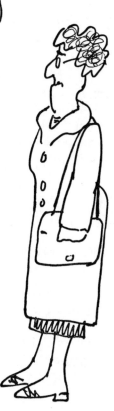

ED FISCHER

Elder reality:

A woman with "no taste" used to mean she had a
purple mohair overstuffed sofa in her parlor.

Now it means she can't tell if there's too much garlic
in her spaghetti sauce.

Metaphor:

Q.: What do you call a bunch of old birds who winter
in Delray Beach?

A.: Migrating blueheads.

Stargazing at seventy:

The Little Dipper reminds you to take your Metamucil.

To December bride, displaying her trousseau:

"Isn't that negligee rather sheer for someone your age?"

"Well, maybe. But at *his* age, Arthur can't see well
enough to notice."

Porch talk:

"Did you hear how Mulligan conned the Medi-cab
    driver into dropping him at the golf club?"

"No. How'd he do that?"

"He told him he had a large handicap!"

Want ad in an Arizona weekly:

Wanted: Bonded escort, silver-haired (not dyed),
    two days a week for three active ladies eighty-plus.
    Should look rich (but not too rich). Politically
    conservative. Good bridge player and waltzer.
    Sharp enough to handle six Bingo cards at once.
    Prefer chauffeur's license, L.P.N., and Black Belt
    in Karate.

You know you're getting old when:

You can't find your glasses without your glasses.

"I refuse to admit that I am more than fifty-two, even if
            that does make my sons illegitimate."
                            — Nancy Astor

> "Worrying about the past is like trying to make birth control pills retroactive."
> — Joey Adams in *Strictly for Laughs*

Yuk:

Riddle: What do you call a history of the romantic escapades of a traveling baseball official?

Answer: "The Rise and Fall of the Roamin' Umpire."

Senior awareness:

"Opal discovered at eighty-nine and a half that she's an Adult Child of a Dysfunctional Family. Now she's going to four recovery groups a week, trying to get enough insights to heal herself and all sixty-two of her descendants by her ninetieth birthday!"

Serious cosmetic need:

"I can't get by with ordinary household face creams anymore. I need Elizabeth Arden in a Drum!"

Community activities director to L.S.W.:

"You see those guys on the shuffleboard court? They
burn their old Jockey briefs. Then they give a
trophy to the one who comes up with the wildest
boxers! You should see those undershorts—
Hawaiian florals, tiger stripes, sea cows, color
prints of old movie queens. Anything goes!"

"What do they call all this?"

"The Boxer Rebellion."

Aside in a supermarket:

"Alice is determined to stay young at all costs. She
buys only foods with preservatives."

You know you're getting old when:

"...you stoop to tie your shoelaces and ask yourself,
What else can I do while I'm down here?"
— George Burns

How's that again?

Two elders meet on a street corner downtown. One
says to the other, "Gosh, I haven't seen you in
years. I can't seem to remember—was it you
or your brother who died?"

our only handicap is that just about everyone under 65 thinks we're handicapped
ED FISCHER

More older-than-thou one-upsmanship:

"I'm so old, I didn't grow up; I evolved."

"I'm so old, the prints of my immediate ancestors aren't in a family album; they're in a layer of sandstone in the Grand Canyon."

Hazard:

"Since Gloria turned eighty, she's become a real menace behind the wheel! The way she barrels around those hills and swerves all over the place!"

"She's really rude to other drivers too."

"She's a threat, all right. I wouldn't be caught on the same fairway with her!"

New haunts for oldsters:

Our hangouts used to be the sports bar and the coffee shop.
Now they're the pharmacy and the bathroom.

"Old people shouldn't eat health foods. They need all the preservatives they can get."
— Robert Orben

Some strategies for women who want to seem younger than they are:

Have your wattle removed surgically.

Keep your electrolysis appointments. (Just because you can't see your "unwanted hair" anymore doesn't mean it isn't there.)

Wear running shoes or at least K-Mart tennies. (Everybody looks younger in tennies.)

Wear a warm-up suit when you're grocery shopping.

Keep a tennis racquet in your car. (You don't have to play—just look as if you're about to.)

Fake a blank look when a contemporary asks if you remember Major Bowes, "Your Hit Parade," Wayne King, or Joe Penner and his duck. (This is tricky—if you look too blank about *too* many things, you'll be the subject of gossip about your memory loss, not your comparative youth.)

When people stop by, be prepared to make a strategic dial switch from your easy-listening Golden Oldies (Mel Torme or Dinah Shore) to a light rock station (Dan Fogelberg or the Beatles). Avoid serious rock—you don't want to drive them away by blasting them with Guns 'n' Roses.

Cancel your subscription to *Mature Wisdom*—or peel
off the address label and put the magazine in your
neighbor's mailbox. (Read it first.)

Give your fifty-year-old strapless prom dress to the
historical society—anonymously.

Pass off your great-grandchildren as your grandchildren. (The older your friends are, the more
confused they are about who's in what generation
anyway.)

One of the few possible
ways to stop aging

Freezer

PEAS
CORN
TV DINNER

ED FISCHER

Some strategies for men who want to seem younger than they are:

Be sure you don't spill out any antique golf balls from the bottom of your bag onto the putting green— those unravelers left over from the '30s that trailed endless skinny ribbons of rubber when they split.

Curb your habit of humming "Good-night, Irene" and "Don't Sit under the Apple Tree with Anyone Else but Me" when you chamois the dew from your sedan in the parking lot.

Offer your white bucks to the Goodwill. (The contents of your closets give away your chronology, especially that moth-masticated letter sweater with the old English "B" in gold felt.)

Don't refer to your wife and her friends as "the girls." (Risky—some feminists are getting old now, too.)

Don't wolf-whistle. That went out years ago.

Change barbers. Your old one knows you too well to try to talk you into a new look. Besides, he may just happen to tell his other customers how old you are!

Middle Age:

"—when your wife tells you to pull in your stomach and you already have."

— Jack Barry

Riddle:

Why do half the retirees in this country move south
into the sun and then do everything they can to stay
out of it?

(Palm trees, cabanas, patio umbrellas, 30-plus
sunscreen lotion, duck-billed visors, enormous
straw hats, newspapers, nose guards, etc.)

Elderfib:

"Sara Jane told her granddaughter that AARP meant
American Alliance of Rollerblading Professionals!"

Bear in mind:

"Lack of pep is often mistaken for patience."
— Indiana humorist Kin Hubbard

You know you're getting old when:

The bus driver calls you "ma'am" instead of "hey, lady!"

Remember:

"After a certain age, if you don't wake up aching in
every joint, you are probably dead."
— Tommy Mein

alas, you could be right—
as you get
older, the ol'
brain starts to
fade fast...
...checkmate
ED FISCHER

Teens, appalled at the limits of their grandmother's vocabulary:

"I asked Gam if she knew what 'heavy metal' was—and you know what she said?"

"No. What?"

"The lid on the dumpster!"

Hobbies and pursuits, by decades:

TEENS: biology

TWENTIES: sociology

THIRTIES: psychology

FORTIES: astrology

FIFTIES: cosmetology

SIXTIES: endocrinology

SEVENTIES: theology

"You know how to tell when you're getting old?
When your broad mind changes places
with your narrow waist!"
— Red Skelton

Frustration in the fourposter:

"The doctor told us we should try to reactivate our
    love life. So I asked Herbert if he remembered
    how he used to nibble my ear—thinking that was
    a start anyway."

"Did it work?"

"No. Herbert took all the romance out of it by getting
    out of bed to go after his teeth!"

Goals:

"I *have* to live to be a hundred. I'm booked!"
— George Burns

Side benefits of forgetting names and faces:

You keep meeting new people every day!

"My grandmother's 90. She's dating.
He's 93. It's going great. They never argue.
They can't hear each other."
— Cathy Ladman

Alternative energy source:

AARP has an incredible resource they need to develop—the candles on the birthday cakes of their members could heat all the dwellings south of the Mason-Dixon line!

Old habits die hard:

"Johnny's a charmer. At eighty-eight, he hasn't forgotten *how* to chase after women. He's just forgotten *why* he does it."

Latter-life crisis:

"Everybody's down on Holcum. His latest fling is twenty-four years younger than he is. She's only seventy-one!"

"Holcum always was one to rob the cradle!"

"Long after we're wearing bifocals or hearing aids, we'll be making love. But we won't know with whom."
— Jack Paar

"I'm at the age now where just putting my cigar in its holder is a thrill."
— George Burns

ED FISCHER

Dilemma:

Perched in my shorts on the edge of my bed,
With a shoe in my hand and my teeth in a cup,
I'm looking for clues, so I don't have to ask:
Am I going to bed now or just getting up?

J.T.N.

"You've heard of the three ages of man—youth, age, and
'you're looking wonderful.'"
— Francis Joseph, Cardinal Spellman

"Youth would be an ideal state if it came
a little later in life."
— Lord Asquith

Observation in a clinic waiting room:

"I wonder how many doctors believe they've cured
their patients, when really those patients just gave
up and went home?"

"A man has reached middle age when he is warned
to slow down by his doctor instead of the police."
— Henny Youngman

Liability or asset?

"Jerome has an elder complex."

"You mean he's got a problem with getting old?"

"No. He owns a senior high-rise."

Breathy aside at a Staying in Shape for Seniors class:

"We should get Shirley (puff) into this class (puff)."

"She'd never do it (puff). The only things she ever
exercises are her rights!"

Speculating teens around the pool during spring vacation:

"Is it true that old people don't sweat?"

"Maybe they just don't do things that *make*
them sweat."

Have I or haven't I?

As you stand by the fridge's open door,
letting all its cold pour out, you
wonder—did you already eat your lunch?
Or are you just about to?

J.T.N.

You know you're getting old when:

You open your outgoing mail.

Name shortage:

Two octogenarians—aside to each other, after being
    introduced to members of a touring collegiate
    singing group:

"That young man is the *fourth* Doug MacDonald I've
    met in my lifetime."

"Well, sure. We've lived so long we know at least three
    people for every name we ever heard of! No
    wonder we're confused!"

The truth is:

"You have to grow old before somebody will tell you
    that you look young for your age."

— Milton Berle

Clues to people's chronology:

Try these on your evasive friends who lie about their ages. If they recognize these terms, you can guess how long they've been around:

CORDUROY KNICKERS

LEGGINGS

DECCA AND BLUEBIRD

FLOOR SHOWS

MEXICAN JUMPING BEANS

THE BIG APPLE

APPLE MARY

CONGA LINES

ZOOT SUITS

HOBO

LIMBO

SATCHMO

ZEPPO

COCO

MA PERKINS

WPA

FOURBUCKLES

CAPTAIN MIDNIGHT

KATZENJAMMER KIDS

SHMOOS

MIDDIES

THE TWIST

PENFIELD AND SAM

THE NEW LOOK

BILLY ROSE'S AQUACADE

DANCE CARDS

ELEANOR POWELL

ELEANOR ROOSEVELT

ELEANOR HOLM

ELEANOR RIGBY

ELEANOR OF AQUITAINE

BROOMSTICK SKIRTS
(they're back again!)

More chronology clues:

Now ask what the word SHAG means:

"A rug." (She's at least sixty.)

"What you tell your dog when you throw a stick for him." (He's probably over seventy.)

"A dance." (She's got to be eighty-plus!)

Elder couple in the midst of a tiff:

"You're impossible! You're going to drive me to an early grave!"

"No, honey. It's a bit late for that!"

Widowers' exchange:

"What do you look for in a woman at our age?"

"Ankles and assets!"

> "Middle age is when you ask the barber
> to thicken it a little on the top."
> — Henny Youngman

Two ex-bankers in a sauna:

"These days, there's only one thing you can count on
for growth and expansion."

"What's that?"

"Gossip."

Oldster summing up a new relationship:

"Yup. I really love her for what she is—the president of
a billion-dollar soft-drink corporation."

Contradiction:

"Somebody ought to set Horace straight—he seems to
think 'retire' means 'go to bed'!"

The enduring spirit of competition:

Eleanor and Florence, two matriarchs eighty-plus, had
played tennis doubles together for sixty years. A
younger woman (fifty or so) was called to fill in.
Imagine her astonishment when Eleanor pulled her
behind the base line and muttered, "Be sure to hit
the balls to Florence. She has a heart condition."

the meeting of the Happy Arthritics will come to order...
ED FISCHER

You know you're older than most if, to you:

A PRINCESS means Margaret Rose.

CLOSETS are where your hang your clothes, not places you come out of.

THE WORKPLACE is a bench in the basement.

DUAL CAREERS refers to a couple of guys who teach fencing.

BUNNIES are pesky, long-eared little animals in your garden.

A CENTERFOLD is a part on your car that leaks oil.

A GROUPIE is a big, friendly fish.

A FLOPPY DISK is a rubber drain stopper.

A LIVE-IN is a housedress.

FAST FOOD is what you eat during Lent.

MOONING means romantic daydreaming about somebody.

A SCAN means a quick perusal of the newspaper.

SOFTWARE means cotton undies.

A CHIP means a little piece of wood (if it's blue, it's a stock).

HARDWARE means screen-door hooks and hinges.

WORD PROCESSOR means a crackerjack secretary.

MODEM is what you did to the weeds in your back yard.

The old and the faithful:

"My husband will never chase another woman.
    He's too fine, too decent, too old."

— Gracie Allen

Eldertruth:

The older you are, the less you're able to hide your true
    character cosmetically.

You know you're getting old when:

That attractive woman on the bus tour sits down on the
    bench next to you and asks, "Is this your good ear?"

You know you're getting old when:

The license bureau informs you that the car you're
    driving (a LaSalle) qualifies for classic plates.

More older-than-thou one-upmanship:

"I'm so old I had Rudy Valentino's tintype under
　　my pillow."

"I'm so old the RCA Victor dog was my puppy."

Declaration on a gamboling senior's T-shirt:

I'm retired. Having fun is my job.

Comfort for a retiring CEO:

You're no longer Top Banana,
but you can still be the tarantula
that raises heck with the bunch!

"At my age, when a girl flirts with me in the movies,
she's after my popcorn."
— Milton Berle

"If I had my life to live over, I'd live
over a delicatessen."
— Unknown

Immortality:

"How does it feel to be the mother of a United States
Senator, a nationally known author, an opera star,
and a lottery winner?"

"I'm not a mother—I'm a historic site!"

*Post-midnight phone call from a resident in a
health-care facility:*

Ninety-year-old southern-born lady to her son, aged
sixty-six:

"Is this mah son?"

"Yes, it is."

"Is this mah son Richahd?"

"Yes. This is your only son Richard."

"Ah have a question."

"Yes?"

"Am ah eighty-nine—or am ah ninety?"

"You're ninety, Mother.

(Thoughtful pause, followed by brief conclusion.)

"Aw! Shoot!"

Material witness:

Your arms are Roman curtains.
Your neck has triple swags.
Your thighs are quilts of folk art.
Your knees are jelly bags.
Your calves fall to your ankles
like the box-pleats on a chair.
Your waist and chest roll into one—
there's so much padding there!
The best disguise: KEEP COVERED
from your chin down to the floor.
Then who can know for certain
you're a walking dry goods store?

J.T.N.

Heard in a funeral parlor:

A middle-aged couple waiting in the funeral home's
    foyer to make arrangements for a deceased and
    honored elder, were met by a red-faced funeral
    director. He apologized for the piped-in music.

The melody, richly orchestrated, was "Stranger
    in Paradise."

"Death: a sure cure for insomnia."
— Leonard Louis Levinson

Misheard on the nineteenth hole:

"Well, this week we can only play one day."

"No, Monday's no good. Besides, it's supposed to
be windy."

"Wednesday? That's not great for me. How about
Thursday?"

"I'm thirsty too. Let's have a drink."

All you ever wanted to know about caves—and more:

Exploring formations and forms of life
in each cave, crevasse, and bunker
has turned your diagnostic physician into
the ultimate spelunker.

J.T.N.

Classically uninformed widow:

"Dolly's a real babe in the woods financially. She thinks
'social security' means Fasteeth and Depends!"

You know you're getting old when:

You remember when doorbells buzzed instead
of chiming out little songs.

Generational block:

"Dad thinks 'dysfunctional' means you can fix it with
Milk of Magnesia."

...and a Minnesota interpretation:

"Uncle Yon thinks 'dysfunctional' means 'dis ting
verks.'"

Medical history, in brief:

"Luther had so many stones, they had to call in a
geologist."

Definition of old age:

"You just wake up one morning, and you got it!"
— Moms Mabley

You know you're getting old when:

Your arms are getting shorter—
your legs are growing longer—
your feet are out of sight—
and the middle of your back might as well be
in Chicago!

Ramifications of the Big Lie:

"Charlotte whittles so many years off her age that she's
    made all her daughters illegitimate."

"And that's not the end of it—her grandchildren all
    seem to be the result of teenage pregnancies."

Realization:

"I'm sixty-three and I'm still wondering who I'll be
    when I grow up."

"I don't believe in an afterlife, although I am
    bringing a change of underwear."
    — Woody Allen

Rose-colored bifocals:

The older you are, the smarter you were as a kid.

Elders remarking on a natural sequence:

"From youth to age, they say you go from passion
    to compassion."

"Compassion takes a lot less out of you!"

Eldergoal:

If you can just make it to a hundred, that's all you need
    to do to have distinguished yourself.

Loving behaviors of youth through the decades:

In the 'teens if we engaged in any COURTING
the goal was clear: our steps must never falter
along the rose-strewn path that led directly
from the settee in the parlor to the altar.

In the '20s wicker porch swings were for SPOONING.
To drown our words, we cranked up the Victrola—
to blare its scratchy music through the window—
or set the player piano to plunk out "Nola."

We called it PITCHING WOO in star-struck '30s.
At the movies watching Fred and Ginger's dances,
we sat squeezed into double seats and wondered
if life could *ever* match those screen romances.

In the '40s in our Buicks we went NECKING.
(In wartime termed it WATCHING SUBMARINE RACES.)
We parked in parks, on country roads, in school yards,
till local cops beamed spotlights in our faces!

Those textbooks in the '50s named it PETTING
(distinctly qualified as "light" or "heavy").
It took place well beyond our parents' earshot,
in the back seat of a souped-up Ford or Chevy.

In the '60s LOVE was everywhere they found it—
impulsive acts performed with no auditions.
Our flower-children children went to Woodstock
and dropped their clothes and all their inhibitions.

In the '70s and '80s BEING ACTIVE,
became—sex-wise—a synonym for scary.
They kept their attitudes and bedroom doors half open,
but health was on their minds, and youth was wary.

Now, looking back, our rumble seats had drawbacks,
and porch-swing spooning *never* kept our backs warm,
but SCORING was, for us, reserved for hockey—
and MAKING OUT meant filling in a tax form!

Though terms may change, each youthful generation
thinks they invented sex—down to the letter!
How stunned they are to learn that we, their elders,
have seen it all before—and DONE IT BETTER!

J.T.N.

Morning memory jog, upon arising:

It's gotten so I have to put
a sign beside my bed:
"First the pants, THEN the shoes!"
It helps me keep my head.

R.T.N.

Clinical exchange:

Elder patient: "Doctor, I have a little foot problem."

Doctor: "I wouldn't worry about it."

Elder patient: "Well, if you had a little foot problem, I
probably wouldn't worry about it either!"

Governmental lapse:

"Fanny is sort of upset. She just got a notice from the
Social Security Administration informing her that
she's dead—and she doesn't know whether to try to
prove she isn't or let it go and wait until she is."

> "Early to rise and early to bed makes a male
> healthy, wealthy, and dead."
> — James Thurber

Try this kitchen note out on a grandchild for translation:

1. Please leave the card in the summer kitchen window for the iceman (empty the icebox pan).

2. Slice up some spuds to fry in the spider.

3. Brew a pot from the best caddy and heat up the johnny cake (the cozy is hanging on the line).

4. Listen for the Daintyman's bell and run out to meet him (there's a nickel for you on the console— or maybe on the hall tree—next to the streetcar tokens).

5. If the horse plow comes to do the sidewalk, give the horse a carrot (you'll find it in the root cellar).

6. Oh, and please clean out the clinkers (use the scuttle).

Even a dancin' fool is not foolish:

"You're asking me to slamdance? Young lady, you're looking at someone who's done the Cakewalk, the Dipsy Doodle, the Big Apple, the Charleston, the Bunny Hop, the Shag, the Continental, the Carioca, the Stomp, the Lindy Hop, the Twist, and the Mashed Potato. But a slamdance at my age could easily turn into a break dance!"

You know you're getting old when:

A game of backgammon feels like a stress test.

Eldersmile:

Q.: What's the opposite of a friendly senior citizen?
A.: An Elderhostel.

Unanswerable question posed to the host of a senior talk show:

"I want to know if it's okay to keep tinting my hair when my forty-eight-year-old daughter's decided to go gray?"

And someone once said:

"Middle Age: When a woman's hair starts turning from gray to black."

Everything
in this
kitchen
has been
determined
to be
hazardous
to your heath

ED FISCHER

Things that twenty years ago you never thought you'd find yourself doing:

Mall-walking

Eating seven bananas a week

Wearing more gold in your mouth than you do on the rest of your body

Meeting your friends over free day-old cookies and coffee at the bank on Fridays

Microwaving everything you eat

Getting hooked on TV soaps

Not reading much after the sun goes down

Taking calcium

Worrying about your cholesterol level

Worrying about your bank account

Worrying about making too much money and losing your social security

Worrying about your friends—they're so darn OLD!

Carrying a huge, lightweight shopping bag everywhere

Wearing bathing suits with skirts—again

Going to the grocery store on the days they give out free samples

Riding buses with herds of others your age

Joining an "elderobics" class

Terms, no longer useful, to strike from senior vocabularies:

BUTLER'S PANTRY: An architectural deletion.

VERANDA: Young ones think it has to do with truth in advertising.

KNOBBY: Once you talked about a "knobby (fancy) hat." Now it can only apply to knees. Don't confuse yourself. Let it go.

NIBLICK: Only very old golfers may recognize this as a nine iron.

ICEBOX: People will know what you mean, but it sure does date you!

FANCY WOMAN: Also "lady of the night." Both are obsolete.

ANTIMACASSAR: They'll think it's your Scotch aunt. Besides, you can now Scotchguard® your upholstery and you don't need little crocheted protectors.

CHEESECAKE: Neither the real stuff from Lindy's or the metaphor for leggy girl pin-ups is around anymore. (The latter went out with the Women's Movement.)

GOING STEADY: One more step and she was "pinned."

RUNNING BOARDS: No, Junior, not skateboards—the little step-up that helped us climb into the old automobiles. Now rare—since human legs are longer and cars are lower-slung and McDonald's and Burger King have done away with the need for the exterior picnic trunk.

GAMS: Formerly "legs," as in "nice gams!" Now, "grandmothers." (These may even *be* "nice gams" who *have* "nice gams!")

You know you're getting old when:

You wear a Jack Armstrong Hike-o-Meter to measure
   your distance while mall-walking.

About a bank-shy elder:

"When she wants to freeze a few of her assets, she just
   stuffs her money in a drawer in her refrigerator
   underneath a head of lettuce and the tomatoes."
                                          — Erma Bombeck

New angle for an angler:

"Gerald has a penchant for catching enormous fish."

"What a great company to retire from! Whoever heard
   of getting a pension just to go fishing!"

You know you're getting old when:

Your head makes promises your body can't possibly
   keep.

Sound and structure:

"Mattie's joints sound like the Fourth of July when she moves around."

"I know. She has a good attitude though. She says that, after all these years, things are finally clicking into place for her!"

> "The farther backward you can look, the farther forward you are likely to see."
> — Winston Churchill

A fork in the road:

There are two ways to go once you hit sixty: you can be a warrior or a sage.

If you're a warrior, you fight the passing years with all the time and energy and money you've got left (facelifts, makeup, wrinkle creams, exercise machines—and younger friends).

If you're a sage, you can turn to spiritual matters, keep your old friends, and forget the facelift.

At some point, even warriors give up and become sages.

honor thy father and mother - give them a call once in a while
ED FISCHER

> "If you're old enough to know better,
> you're too old to do it."
> — George Burns

If expressions can date you...

Here are some you don't hear much anymore:

FIDDLESTICKS	MY EYE!
PSHAW!	OH, FOOT!
MERCY ME!	MY LAND!
HEY, TOOTS	LAND SAKES!
EGADS!	GADZOOKS!
GEEZ LOUISE	GLORIOSKY!
HOITY TOITY	TWENTY-THREE SKIDDOO
OH, FOR GOODNESS' SAKE!	OH, BOTHER!
WANNA BUY A DUCK?	HEAVENS TO MURGATROYD!

A partner with pace:

"Gert's a great dancer. She's got terrific rhythm. But I just can't keep up with her."

"Why not?"

"She's got wheels on her walker."

Evolutions:

Lounge lizards have become couch potatoes
Rumble seats have become hatchbacks
Woodies have become vans
Trailers have become mobile homes
Iceboxes have become refrigerators
Stoves have become ranges
Lanterns have become flashlights
Fourposters have become queen-sized waterbeds
Roads have become freeways
Ragtime has become rock
Hopscotch has become break dancing
Work-at-home males have become house-husbands
Garbagemen have become sanitary engineers
Janitors have become environmental serenity specialists
Simps have become wimps
Saps have become jerks
Secretaries have become administrative assistants
Plumbers have become rich
And, most amazing of all, WE HAVE BECOME OLD!

Remarks we could easily get tired of hearing:

"You're doing well—for your age."

"You're not getting any younger, you know."

"You're just remarkable!" (Meaning: How can you do what you do when you're so old?)

"Well, at this point, it probably won't kill you." (About an ailment diagnosed late in life.)

"Are you really *that* old? You sure don't show it."

"You're pretty spry for your age."

"You're so cute!" (When you've never been cute in your life, "cute" is a synonym for "old.")

"You'll probably outlive us all." (From a thirty-two-year-old doctor. Small chance!)

Grow old along with me?

"I'm growing old by myself. My wife hasn't had a birthday in years."

— Milton Berle

Riddle:

Q.: What's the most inexpensive, most creative, most enduring toy of all?

A.: A grandparent.

Another riddle:

Q.: What tree and what bush describe the business activities of a funeral home?

A.: Box elder and elderberry.

One of life's greatest mysteries:

"The guy who wasn't smart enough to marry my daughter is the parent of the smartest grandchild in the world!"

— Joey Adams

"Children are a great comfort in your old age—and they help you reach it faster, too."

— Lionel Kauffman

Sounds we don't hear much anymore:

Parlor pump organs

Steam radiators knocking

Steam locomotives

Gas jets

The Good Humor man's horse snorting in the street

A telephone operator saying, "Number pleeaz."

Serial puffing on tobacco pipes

Newsboys yelling "EXTRA! EXTRA!
  READ ALL ABOUT IT!"

Railroad cars coupling and uncoupling in the
  freight yards

Coffee percolating

Empty milk bottles clinking in the milkman's carrier

Ice being chipped with an icepick

Ourselves roaring at our kids

You know you're getting old when:

Your childhood toys turn up in antique malls with huge
  price tags on them.

it's nice raising something that doesn't talk back to you...
Peas
ED FISCHER

Spiritual or practical?

"The minister came to call yesterday. He told me that, since I was getting on in years, I should be thinking about the hereafter."

"So what did you tell him?"

"I said, 'Oh, I do that all the time. Wherever I am—in the kitchen, in the laundry, in the living room, upstairs—I ask myself, Now what is it I'm here after?'"

A hardy octogenarian to his septuagenarian sister:

"It's a wonder we survived our childhood. We teethed on lead paint. We rode out diptheria, scarlet fever, the measles, and whooping cough. You hit me over the head with a cast-iron dump truck, and I flipped a jack knife into your palm while playing mumblety-peg. And now they worry about kids swallowing plastic eyes from stuffed toys!"

Extreme measure of secrecy:

"Lois doesn't travel overseas, you know. She refuses to apply for a passport because she'd have to bring in her birth certificate and divulge her true age."

What do we like to be called?

Newsweek, April 23, 1990, cited these possibilities:

WHOOPIES (Well-Heeled Older People)

OPALS (Older Persons with Active Lifestyles)

GRUMPIES (Grown-up Mature People)

Here are a few more:

OOMPAS (Old Or Mature Persons with Affluence and Status)

SAGES (Senior Adults Growing in Excellence and Spirituality)

GOLDIES (Great Old Love-Directed Individuals with Energy and Sagacity)

MARCERS (Mature Adults Responding with Care, Experience, and Resources)

or:

PRIME TIMERS	SECOND CAREERISTS
POST-MIDSTERS	SENIOR CONSULTANTS

What we don't like to be called (what we are not!):

Old fogeys, codgers, crones, old men, old women, old farts, dodderers in our dotage, retirees (we retire from some things but get into others), oldsters (sounds like an antique touring car), has beens (no way—we're still about-to-be's!)

Minor senior crises—or Grandmother O'Murphy's Laws:

Your shower will overflow and cause a flood in all the apartments directly below you—when your neighbor three stories down is having her annual luncheon for her hospital volunteers group.

Your tax figures will blow into the pool on April 14.

The minister or rabbi will stop by on the day you've hired Nozzle Nolen (the fumigators) to get rid of the palmetto bugs.

You will sprain your toe just before the senior square dance.

Your golf cart will stall in the middle of the fairway 150 yards from the tenth tee.

Somebody will swipe your bowling ball on the eve of the league tournament.

Your doctor will move to a different town just as she's getting to the bottom of your intestinal flare-ups.

You finally find a medicine that works for you and it makes you itch.

Your car won't start on the morning of your first meeting with a client who's hired you as a free-lance consultant. (Like dogs, you can count seven automobile years for every human year. Your twelve-year-old Chrysler is the equivalent of eighty-four!)

(Here, add some of your own. Laugh about these little crises. Complaining just makes you no fun.)

Cultivating the positive images of aging:

How about "wise," "venerable," "experienced," "well-seasoned," "well-tempered," "hardy," dynamic," "energetic," "useful," and "growing spiritually"?

That's us.

Pertinent definition:

Aging is not something that happens to you. It's something you choose to do well.

> "You grow up the day you have your
> first real laugh at yourself."
> — Ethel Barrymore

About the authors

Ed Fischer, whose cartoons first appeared in the *Minneapolis Star and Tribune*, has been a full-time editorial cartoonist with the *Omaha World-Herald* and the *Tulsa Tribune*, and now holds that position with the *Rochester Post-Bulletin* in Minnesota. His cartoons, syndicated in seventy-five newspapers, have been reprinted in *Time, Newsweek,* and *U.S. News and World Report,* as well as in many other publications. He is the recipient of twenty-five awards, including the Overseas Press Club award, one of the highest honors in his profession.

He is the author of eight books, including *Minnesota, A Cold Love Affair,* and *101 Things to Do with Lutefisk.*

Jane Thomas Noland, a former feature writer and children's books editor for the *Minneapolis Star and Tribune*, is a free-lance writer and books editor. She is the author of *Laugh It Off, The New Humor Strategy of Weight Loss,* and coauthor, with Dennis D. Nelson, of *Young Winners' Way, A Twelve Step Guide for Teenagers.* She is also coauthor of a classic meditation book, *A Day at a Time,* now with nearly a million in print. Her fiction has been published in *Woman's Day* magazine.

She is a Phi Beta Kappa graduate of Smith College. She and her husband are parents of two grown children and live in Wayzata, Minnesota.